This or That Pets

Is a HAMSTER or a GERBIL the Pet for Me?

by Mari Schuh

raintree
a Capstone company — publishers for children

Raintree is an imprint of Capstone Global Library Limited, a company incorporated in England and Wales having its registered office at 264 Banbury Road, Oxford, OX2 7DY – Registered company number: 6695582

www.raintree.co.uk
myorders@raintree.co.uk

Edited by Carrie Sheely
Designed by Bobbie Nuytten
Original illustrations © Capstone Global Library Limited 2025
Picture research by Jo Miller
Production by Whitney Schaefer

Originated by Capstone Global Library Ltd
978 1 3982 5800 6

British Library Cataloguing in Publication Data
A full catalogue record for this book is available from the British Library.

Acknowledgements
We would like to thank the following for permission to reproduce photographs: Getty Images: Coral Hernandez, 17, Raylipscombe, 10, Skyimages, 9, Sol de Zuasnabar Brebbia, 19; Shutterstock: Aisylu Ahmadieva, 15, AlexKalashnikov, 8, AlmostViralDesign, 4, Billion Photos, 13, Holger Kirk, 7, JessicaGirvan, Cover (top), Kuttelvaserova Stuchelova, 21, Lauren Suryanata, Cover (bottom), marinakarpenko, 5, Natalia Duryagina, 12, Natalya On, 11, Natasha Pankina, background (throughout), Pixel-Shot, 6, ToNN Stocker, 14, Tsekhmister, 20

Every effort has been made to contact copyright holders of material reproduced in this book. Any omissions will be rectified in subsequent printings if notice is given to the publisher.

All the internet addresses (URLs) given in this book were valid at the time of going to press. However, due to the dynamic nature of the internet, some addresses may have changed, or sites may have changed or ceased to exist since publication. While the author and publisher regret any inconvenience this may cause readers, no responsibility for any such changes can be accepted by either the author or the publisher.

Printed and bound in India.

Contents

Words in **bold** are in the glossary.

Getting a new pet

Long whiskers. Cute faces. Fluffy fur. Gerbils and hamsters are fun, popular pets. They look a lot alike. But they are different animals. Find out which pet might be best for you!

gerbil

hamster

How they look

Look closely! Hamsters and gerbils are not the same. Hamsters are rounder. They stuff food into their chubby cheeks. Hamsters have short legs. Their tails are short too.

Gerbils are longer and thinner
than hamsters. They have longer tails.
Gerbils often stand up on their back legs.

Day or night activity?

Do you want a pet that sleeps when you do? Hamsters might not be the best for you. They are most active, and are loudest at night. If the hamster cage is in your bedroom, you might find it hard to sleep.

Gerbils often have naps. They sleep for a few hours at a time. Some sleep during the day. Some sleep at night. When gerbils are awake, they have lots of energy! They run and play with toys.

What they do

How do hamsters and gerbils spend their time? Hamsters often run on an exercise wheel. They dig and make **burrows**. Hamsters might build their nests quickly. Then they rest.

Gerbils tend to be more active. They spend a lot of time digging. Gerbils chew and nibble. They jump and play in their cage. They are fun to watch!

Cuddly or not?

Many owners like to hold and **cuddle** their pets. Hamsters move slowly, so they are quite easy to hold. But they do not like being held for a long time. They might bite if they are scared.

Gerbils are fast. This can make them harder to hold. But gerbils are usually okay with being held. They are less likely to bite.

One or more?

Would you like one pet or a pair? Most hamster **breeds** do better if they live alone. If two hamsters live together, they might fight. It is best to have only one hamster.

Gerbils do not like to live alone. They can get **lonely**. They need to live with one or two other gerbils. They often cuddle and sleep together.

Training

Hamsters and gerbils are clever! With time and work, gerbils can be trained to sit in a person's hand. They can learn to use a **litter tray**. Gerbils can learn tricks. They can jump into your hand. They can learn to come to you when you say their name.

Hamsters can learn tricks too. But not as many as gerbils.

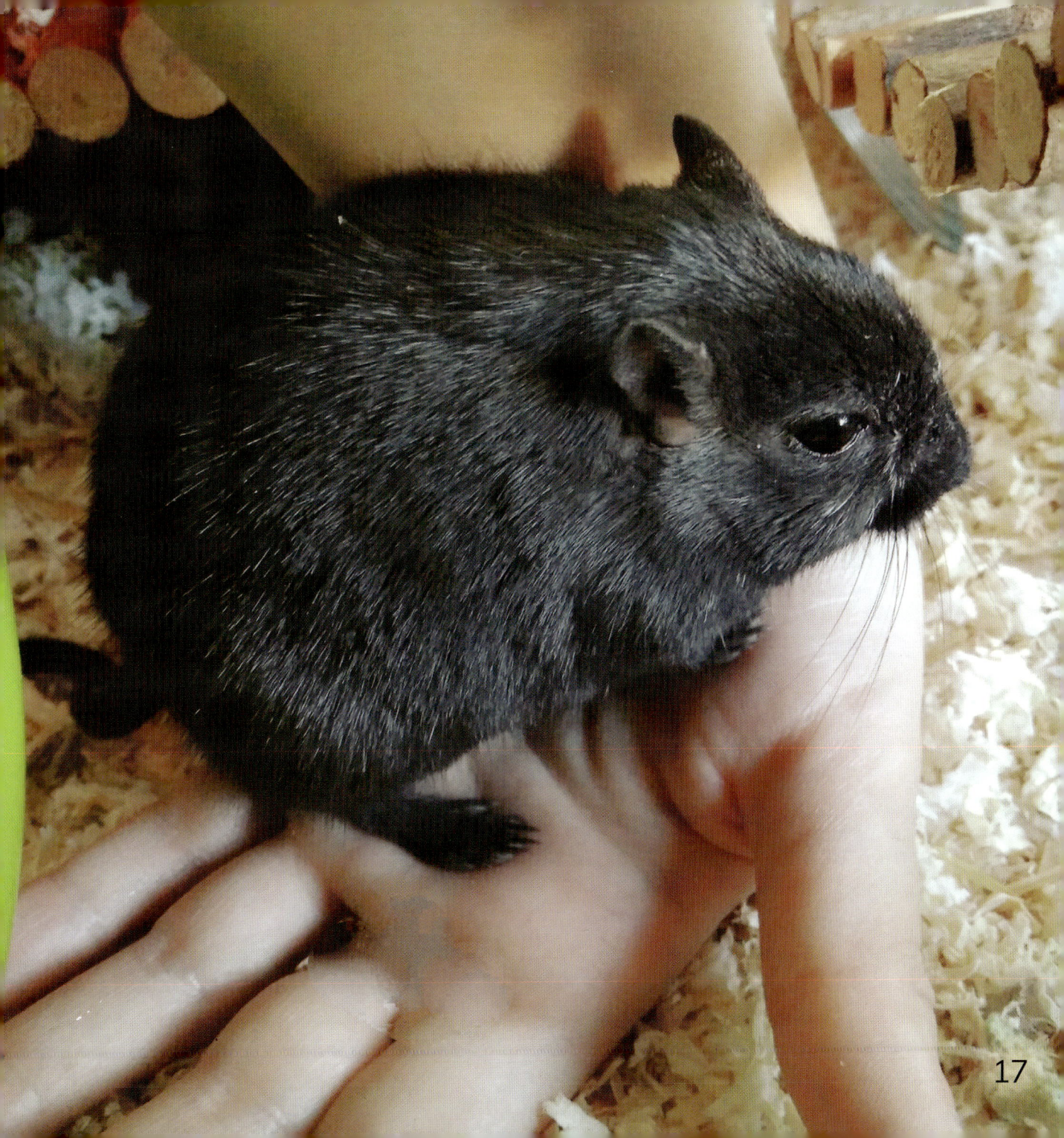

Short lives

Both hamsters and gerbils have short lives. Hamsters usually live for one or two years. Gerbils can live longer. Some gerbils live for three to five years.

Both hamsters and gerbils need good care. Having a pet can be hard work. It takes time to give them happy, healthy lives.

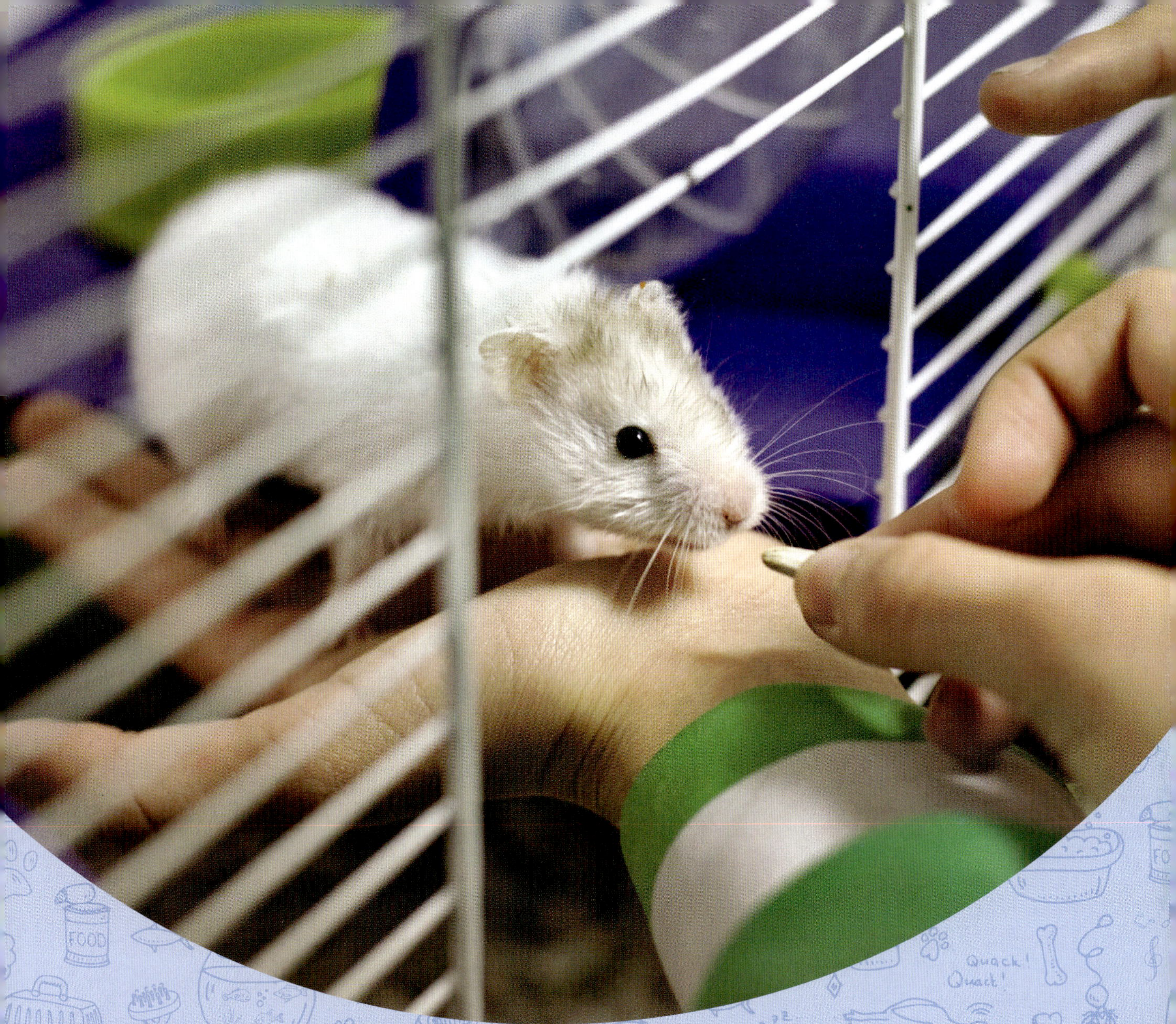

Which pet is best for you?

There is no perfect pet for everyone. The best pet for you might not be the best pet for someone else. This activity can help you find out whether a hamster or gerbil might be best for you and your family.

What you need:

- pencil, pen or marker pen

- two pieces of paper

- small toys

What you do:

1. Write the word "gerbil" on one piece of paper. On the other piece of paper, write the word "hamster".

2. Put the two pieces of paper on the floor.

3. Read the different chapter titles in this book. For each one, think about whether a hamster or gerbil would be the best fit for you. Place a toy in a pile near the piece of paper that best matches your answer. For example, if "gerbil" is your answer, put a toy near the piece of paper that says "gerbil".

4. When you have finished, count the number of toys in each pile. Do you have more toys in the hamster pile? Or do you have more toys in the gerbil pile? Which pet is better for you?

Glossary

breed certain kind of animal within an animal group

burrow tunnel or hole made or used by an animal

cuddle hug and hold

litter tray container indoors for a pet to wee and poo in

lonely feeling alone and sad

Find out more

Books

Caring for Hamsters (Expert Pet Care), Tammy Gagne (Raintree, 2018)

National Geographic Readers: Squeak! 100 Fun Facts about Hamsters, Mice, Guinea Pigs and More, Rose Davidson (National Geographic Kids, 2019)

Websites

kids.britannica.com/kids/article/hamster/400292
Find out more about hamsters with Britannica Kids.

kids.kiddle.co/gerbil
Discover more about gerbils.

kids.nationalgeographic.com/nature/article/wild-hamsters
Learn all about hamsters, from in the wild to your bedroom.

Index

About the author

Mari Schuh's love of reading began with cereal boxes at the kitchen table. Today, she is the author of hundreds of non-fiction books for early readers. Mari lives with her husband and their cheeky house rabbit. Learn more about her at marischuh.com.